THE CHILDREN'S BIBLE

Volume 6

A Golden Press / Funk & Wagnalls, Inc. Book
Published by Western Publishing Company, Inc.

COPYRIGHT © 1981, 1965 BY WESTERN PUBLISHING COMPANY, INC. COPYRIGHT © 1962 BY FRATELLI FAB-BRI, MILAN, ALL RIGHTS RESERVED. PRINTED IN THE U.S.A. PUBLISHED BY GOLDEN PRESS, NEW YORK, BY ARRANGEMENT WITH WESTERN PUBLISHING—HACHETTE INTERNATIONAL, S.A., GENEVA. GOLDEN® AND GOLDEN PRESS® are trademarks of Western Publishing Company, Inc.

Classic™ binding
R. R. Donnelley & Sons Company
patents--U.S. pending

Distributed by Funk & Wagnalls, Inc. New York

Library of Congress Catalog Card Number: 81-81439

ISBN 0-8343-0043-5 (Volume 6)
ISBN 0-8343-0037-0 (12 Volume Set)

CONTENTS

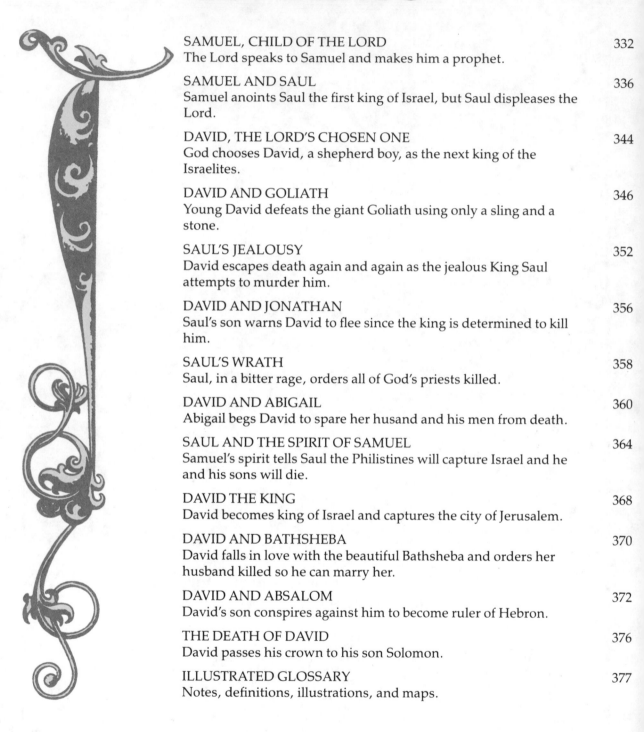

INTRODUCTION

After the Israelites conquered Canaan, its land was divided among the Twelve Tribes, and the people of Israel settled down and became farmers and shepherds. Each of the Twelve Tribes of Israel ruled its own small part of the land. The tribes ruled separately and only met together once a year, to pray at the shrine in Shiloh.

Since the tribes of Israel did not act together as a united nation they did not have a common army, even though they were surrounded by powerful enemies like the Philistines. Fighting separately, the tribes were no match for the fierce Philistines. The story of the long wars that the Israelites fought against the Philistines, and their efforts to unite against their common enemy, is told in the two Books of Samuel.

The Philistines first attacked the Israelites around the year 1050 B.C. They swooped down in fast chariots made of iron, and they carried terrible weapons. The Israelites fought bravely, but were overpowered by the savage Philistines. The Philistines destroyed the great shrine at Shiloh where the Israelites worshipped God. They killed the priests and stole the Ark of the Covenant. The Philistines took over the land and dominated the Israelites.

The people of Israel cried to God for help during this dark time. God heard their prayer. God helped all the children of Israel by helping a sad childless woman named Hannah. He gave Hannah a son, Samuel, whom he chose to lead and serve the people of Israel. Samuel was a man of God and he did what the Lord wanted him to do.

The people asked the prophet Samuel to choose a king to lead them. Even though all the nations around Israel had kings, Israel had never before had a king. It was a new idea for Israel to have a king, but the rulers of the Twelve Tribes knew that their people had to fight as one nation if they were to defeat the Philistines, and they needed a king to unite them.

Samuel was not sure whether he should grant the people's request. He knew that Israel had never had a king because the people believed that God ruled their land. They had not needed a king because God was their friend and protector. Samuel was afraid that God would be angered by the people's wish to have a king. He was worried that God would feel that the people did not trust him. Samuel also worried that if the people had a king, soon they would begin thinking that they did not need God anymore.

So Samuel looked to God for guidance, and God granted the people their wish: he told Samuel to anoint the young man Saul as king of the Israelites. The people followed Saul, not because he was a great warrior or a powerful chieftain, but because they believed that God was with him. The people believed that when a man was anointed, God gave him special power.

Saul had to defend Israel against the powerful armies of the Philistines. He was a good and brave soldier and his troops loved him. He began to push the Philistines out of Israel. Just as Samuel had feared, however, Saul soon became very proud and disobeyed God. Saul thought that he could rule the nation of Israel by himself. Samuel became so angry with Saul that he left him. Saul soon discovered that leading the fight against the Philistines was a very hard task, too difficult to do alone. He was overcome with sadness and loneliness. He began to distrust the people close to him, thinking that everyone wanted to kill him.

The Philistines defeated Saul's army at the battle of Gilboa. When Saul saw what had happened to his army he killed himself in despair, and the Philistines captured his body and showed it to all the Israelites to frighten them. The Philistines once again controlled the Israelites. It seemed as though the Israelites would never be free.

Yet God did not abandon his people. He chose David to be king of Israel. David was a poor shepherd boy from the town of Bethlehem. The Bible tells us that when Saul was fighting against the Philistines, David came to do battle with the giant Philistine warrior, Goliath. David was a young boy when he fought Goliath. Saul's soldiers laughed at him when he told them he wanted to fight the giant. They told him that he was just a boy. But David showed them how brave he was—he went out alone and killed Goliath and saved the Israelite army.

David was the greatest king of ancient Israel. At first David ruled only the southern part of Israel, which was called Judah. After Saul's death he united all the tribes into one great nation, and became king of both the north and the south of Israel. David led the Israelites against the Philistines. His army crushed the Philistines in a terrible battle near Jerusalem. The Philistines promised to obey David from that time on and they never troubled Israel again. David turned Israel into an empire as great as Egypt's. He defeated all of Israel's enemies and captured their land. Under the leadership of King David, Israel became one of the greatest powers of the world.

David governed his empire from his court in Jerusalem. He captured the city from the Canaanites, and he made it his capital since it was located near the center of Israel. Jerusalem was built on two high hills so that it was easy to defend against enemies. It had a good water supply. Today the beautiful city of Jerusalem is still a special place for Jews, Christians, and Muslims.

The children of Israel loved King David because he was a man of God. The people believed that the Lord's spirit rested on David. They said that God helped David in everything he did. Most of the time he obeyed God's wishes; however, David was not always a kind and gentle king. David reminded the people that they should worship God and be grateful to him. David brought the Ark of the Covenant to Jerusalem and he set up Israel's shrine, which had been destroyed by the Philistines, in his capital city. On the day when the Ark was brought into the city, David and the Israelites danced for joy in the streets. They believed that God too would now rule from Jerusalem.

When David became king of Israel his people were still dominated by the Philistines, but by the time David died, Israel had become a great empire. Israel was still bound by the promise that Moses and his people had made to God at Sinai. God would help Israel and protect it only if the people kept his law. He wanted Israel to be a special nation and to show all the other nations of the world how men and women should live in obedience to God. This was Israel's great challenge: as the nation of Israel became stronger and stronger, would the people always remember God and keep his commandments?

Throughout the stories in the books of Samuel, God takes poor and humble men and women, such as Hannah, Saul, and David, and makes them part of his plan for Israel. Jews and Christians believe that even today God asks men and women, boys and girls, to help him with his plans for the world.

from the BOOKS OF I SAMUEL and II SAMUEL

SAMUEL CHILD OF THE LORD

ONCE there was a woman named Hannah who was bitter in her soul because she had no sons or daughters. She prayed to the Lord and wept sadly. And she vowed a vow:

"O Lord of hosts, if you will look down upon the sadness of your handmaiden and remember me, and will give to your handmaiden a man child, then I will give him to the Lord all the days of his life, and no razor shall touch his head."

It came to pass in due time that Hannah bore a son, and she called him Samuel, "Because," she said, "I asked him of the Lord."

Her husband Elkanah, and all his household, went up to offer to the Lord the yearly sacrifice. But Hannah did not go, for she said to her husband: "I will not go up until the child is weaned, and then I will take him so that he may appear before the Lord and stay there forever."

Elkanah her husband said to her: "Do what seems to you best. Wait until you have weaned him; only keep your word to the Lord." So the woman stayed home and nursed her son until he was old enough to wean.

When she had weaned him, she took him up with her, with a young bull of three years and one measure of flour and a bottle of wine. She brought him to the house of the Lord in Shiloh, when the child was still very young.

And so the young bull was slain and the child was brought to Eli the priest. And Hannah said: "O my lord, I am the woman who stood in the temple here, praying to the Lord. I prayed for this child, and the Lord has given me what I asked of him. Therefore

332

I have lent him to the Lord. As long as he lives he shall be lent to the Lord."

Then they worshiped the Lord there. And when Elkanah and his household went home, Samuel stayed, and was taught by Eli the priest.

Each year Samuel's mother made him a little coat and brought it to him when she came up with her husband to offer the yearly sacrifice.

And the child Samuel grew, and was in favor both with the Lord and with men. And he ministered to the Lord before Eli.

GOD CALLS SAMUEL

Eli's eyes began to grow dim, so that he could not see. Once, when Eli was lying down in his place, before the lamp of God was put out in the temple where the ark of the Lord was kept, and before Samuel had lain down to sleep, God called Samuel, and he answered: "Here I am."

And Samuel ran to Eli and said: "Here I am; you called me."

Eli said: "I did not call. Lie down and sleep."

He went and lay down, and again God called: "Samuel."

Samuel arose and went to Eli and said: "Here I am, for you called me."

And Eli answered: "I did not call, my son; lie down again."

Now Samuel did not yet recognize the Lord, nor had the voice of the Lord been made known to him.

And God called Samuel again the third time, and he arose and went to Eli and said: "Here I am, for you called me."

Then Eli understood that the Lord had called the child. So Eli said to Samuel: "Go and lie down, and if he calls you, you are to say: 'Speak, Lord, for your servant is listening.' "

So Samuel went and lay down in his place.

And God came and stood there, and called as at the other times: "Samuel, Samuel."

Then Samuel answered: "Speak, for your servant is listening."

And then God said to Samuel: "Behold, I am going to do something in Israel at which the ears of everyone who hears it shall tingle. On an appointed day I will perform against Eli all the things I have spoken of concerning his household" (for Eli's sons were very wicked) "and when I begin I shall finish it. For I have told him that I will judge his house for

you, and more, if you hide anything from me of the things he said to you."

So Samuel told him everything, and hid nothing from him.

Eli said: "It is the Lord: let him do whatever seems good to him."

Samuel grew, and the Lord was with him. And all Israel, from Dan to Beersheba, knew that Samuel was to be a prophet of the Lord.

THE PHILISTINES CAPTURE THE ARK

Now Israel went out to battle against the Philistines. After a bloody day's reverses, the elders of Israel said: "Why has the Lord struck us today before the Philistines? Let us fetch the ark of the covenant of the Lord from Shiloh, so that when it comes among us it may save us from the hand of our enemies."

So the people sent to Shiloh, and when the ark of the covenant of the Lord came into the camp, all Israel shouted with a great shout, so that the earth rang out.

And when the Philistines heard the noise of the shout, they said: "What does this mean, the noise of this great shout in the camp of the Hebrews?"

They learned that the ark of the Lord had come into the camp, and they were afraid, for they said: "God has come into the camp. Woe unto us! This is the god that struck the Egyptians with all the plagues in the wilderness."

But their leaders said: "Be strong and act like men, O Philistines, so that you do not become servants to the Hebrews as they have been to you. Quit yourselves like men and fight."

And the Philistines fought and Israel was defeated. There was a very great slaughter. Thirty thousand of Israel's footmen fell, and the ark of God was taken.

ever for the wickedness of which he knows, because his sons became evil, and he did not restrain them. Therefor I have sworn to the house of Eli that their wickedness shall not be cleansed with sacrifices nor offerings for ever."

Samuel lay until morning. Then he opened the doors of the house of the Lord, but he feared to tell Eli of the vision. Then Eli called Samuel and said: "Samuel, my son."

And he answered: "Here I am."

And Eli said: "What was it that the Lord said to you? I beg you not to hide it from me. May God punish

SAMUEL AND SAUL

AMUEL judged Israel all the days of his life. He went from year to year on circuit to Bethel and Gilgal and Mizpeh and judged Israel in all these places. But his home was in Ramah and there he judged Israel and built an altar unto the Lord.

When Samuel was old he made his sons Joel and Abiah judges over Israel. But they did not walk in his ways, for they took bribes and delivered false judgments.

THE PEOPLE ASK FOR A KING

Then all the elders of Israel gathered themselves together and came to Samuel in Ramah and said to him: "Behold, you are old and your sons do not walk in your ways. Give us a king to judge us, like all the other nations."

Their words displeased Samuel. He prayed to the Lord and God answered, saying: "Listen to the voice of all the people, for it is not you that they have rejected, but me, that I may not reign over them. And as they have forsaken me and served false gods ever since the day that I brought them up out of Egypt, even so do they unto you. So listen to their voice. Nevertheless, make a solemn protest, and show them what kind of a king is going to reign over them."

So Samuel told the people what God had said to him. And he said: "This is the kind of king who will reign over you. He will take your sons to be his charioteers and his horsemen, and to run before his chariots, to till his ground and reap his harvests and to manufacture his weapons and his chariots. He will take your daughters to be his cooks and bakers; your fields will he take and your best vineyards, and olive groves, and give them to his servants. And he will take a tenth part of your grain and of your vintage, and give it to his officers and his servants. He will take your menservants and your maidservants, your best young men and your asses, and put them to work for him. And you will complain and mourn because of this king whom you have chosen, but the Lord will not listen to you."

However, the people refused to obey the voice of Samuel. They said: "No, we want a king like all the other nations, a king to judge us and fight our battles."

Samuel listened and repeated what they had said to the Lord.

And God said to him: "Give them their way and find them a king."

So Samuel said to the men of Israel: "All of you, go back to your own city."

Now there was a Benjamite called Kish, a man of power and standing, and he had a son whose name was Saul. Saul was the most handsome man of Israel, and he stood head and shoulders above all others.

Kish had lost some of his asses, so he said to his son Saul: "Take one of the servants with you, and go and look for my asses."

So Saul traveled across the Mount

Ephraim and through the land of Sha-
lisha and the land of Shalim and the
land of the Benjamites, but he found
no trace of his father's asses.

When they came to the land of Zuph,
Saul said to his servant: "Come, let
us go home, or my father will cease to
think about his asses and begin to
wonder about our own fate. But in this
city there is a man of God, and he is
an honorable man. Let us go to see
him, and perhaps he can show us which
path to follow. Only, if we do consult
him, what shall we bring as a present?
For we have nothing left that is fit for
a man of God."

Saul's servant said: "See, I have the
fourth part of a shekel of silver. We can
give that to the man of God and he will
tell us which way to go."

SAUL MEETS SAMUEL

They went into the city and the maidens at the well told them that Samuel was going to bless a sacrifice that day on the high place, so they went on to the high place and met Samuel on his way there.

The Lord had warned Samuel the day before that a Benjamite was coming to meet him, and that this was the man whom he should anoint king of Israel. When Samuel saw Saul, the Lord said: "Here is the man of whom I spoke, the one who shall reign over my people."

So Samuel spoke to Saul and told him to set his mind no longer upon the lost asses for they had been found. He said: "To whom does Israel look? Is it not to you and all your father's house?"

Saul said: "I am a Benjamite, a member of the smallest of all the tribes of Israel, and my family is the least important in the tribe of Ben-

jamin. Why do you speak to me in this manner?"

Samuel took Saul and his servant and brought them into the parlor and made them sit at the head of the table, above all the other guests, of whom there were about thirty. And Samuel told the cook to serve Saul with the special portion of meat which had been reserved for the guest of honor.

The next day Samuel took a vial of oil, and poured it upon Saul's head and kissed him and said: "Is it not because the Lord has anointed you to be captain of his people?"

Saul went back to his own country, and the Spirit of God came upon him and he prophesied, so that those who knew him before were amazed and said: "What has happened to the son of Kish? Is Saul also one of the prophets?" Saul told his family that he had met a man of God who had told him that the lost asses were found, but, in telling them, he made no mention of his anointing or of the kingdom.

SAUL IS PROCLAIMED KING

Now Samuel called the people together at Mizpeh and said to them: "Thus says the Lord God of Israel, 'I brought Israel out of Egypt and delivered you out of the hand of the Egyptians and out of the hand of all kingdoms and those that oppressed you.' But you have this day rejected your God who himself saved you from your adversities and your tribulations, and you have said to him: 'Nay, but set a king over us.'

"Now therefore present yourselves before the Lord by your tribes and by your thousands." And when Samuel had caused all the tribes of Israel to come near, the tribe of Benjamin was indicated by lot. When he had caused the tribe of Benjamin to come near by families, the family of Matri was indicated, and Saul, the son of Kish, was indicated. But when they sought him, he could not at first be found.

And when they did find him, he was among the baggage. He was brought into the crowd, and when he stood among them he was higher than any of them from his shoulders upward.

And Samuel said: "Look, there is the man whom the Lord has chosen, and there is nobody like him among all the people."

And all the people shouted and said: "God save the king."

Saul became a great king and a mighty man of valor, and he led the children of Israel into many battles against their enemies the Philistines, but after a while he disobeyed the laws of the Lord.

Samuel warned him, saying: "You have been very foolish in not keeping the commandment of the Lord your God, for had you done so, the Lord would have established your kingdom upon Israel for ever. But now your kingdom will not continue."

JONATHAN BREAKS THE OATH

Saul had a son name Jonathan and it came to pass one day in the course of a battle that Saul said to the people: "Cursed be the man that eats any food until evening, that I may be avenged of my enemies." So none of the people tasted any food.

And all they of the land came to a wood and there was honey on the ground. But no man put his hand to his mouth, for the people feared the curse.

But Jonathan did not hear when his father charged the people with the oath. Therefore, he put the end of the rod that was in his hand and dipped it in a honeycomb and put his hand to his mouth.

Then one of the people said, "Your father ordered the people with an oath, saying: 'Cursed be the man that eats any food this day.'" But Jonathan said: "My father has troubled the land."

After a battle with the Philistines, Saul said: "Let us go down after them again by night and fight them until the morning light, and let us not leave a man alive among them."

Saul asked counsel of God: "Shall I go down after the Philistines? Will you deliver them into the hand of Israel?"

But the Lord did not answer him that day. So Saul said: "Draw together all chiefs of the people, and let us see what sin has been done this day. For, as the Lord lives that saves Israel, even if the sin be Jonathan my son's, he shall surely die."

Therefore lots were chosen, first between Saul and Jonathan on one side and the people on the other, and then between Saul and Jonathan. And Jonathan was indicated. Then Saul said to Jonathan, "Tell me what you have done." And Jonathan told him: "I did but taste a little honey with the

end of the rod that was in my hand, and lo, I must die."

And Saul answered: "You shall surely die, Jonathan."

THE PEOPLE RESCUE JONATHAN

Then the people said to Saul: "Shall Jonathan die who has wrought this great salvation in Israel? God forbid. As the Lord lives, there shall not one hair of his head fall to the ground, for he has worked with God this day."

So the people rescued Jonathan and he did not die.

Then Saul went up from following the Philistines, and the Philistines went to their own place.

SAUL DISOBEYS THE LORD

Samuel said to Saul: "The Lord sent me to anoint you to be king over his people, over Israel. Now therefore listen to the voice of the words of the Lord. Thus says the Lord of hosts: 'I remember what Amalek did to Israel, how he laid in wait for him on the road when he came from Egypt. Now go and attack Amalek and utterly destroy all that they have, and do not spare them. But slay both man and woman, child and baby, ox and sheep, camel and ass.'"

Saul struck the Amalekites from Havilah to Shur, near Egypt. He took Agag the king of the Amalekites alive, and utterly destroyed all the people with the edge of the sword. But Saul and the people spared the best of the sheep and of the oxen and of the fatlings, and the lambs and all that was good, and would not destroy them.

But everything that was vile they destroyed utterly.

Then the word of the Lord came to Samuel, saying: "I regret that I have set up Saul to be king. For he has turned back from following me, and has not performed my commandments." And it grieved Samuel, and he cried to the Lord all night.

And Samuel came to Saul, and Saul said to him: "Blessed be you of the Lord. I have performed the commandment of the Lord."

Samuel said: "What means then this bleating of sheep and the lowing of oxen which I hear?"

And Saul said: "They have brought them from the Amalekites, for the people spared the best of the sheep and of the oxen to sacrifice to the Lord your God. And the rest we have destroyed utterly."

Then Samuel said to Saul: "The Lord sent you on a journey and said, 'Go and utterly destroy the sinners, the Amalekites.' Why then did you not obey the voice of the Lord?

"Has the Lord as great delight in burnt offerings and sacrifices as in obeying the voice of the Lord? Behold, to obey is better than to sacrifice, and to listen then the fat of rams. For rebellion is like the sin of witchcraft, and stubbornness is like iniquity and idolatry. Because you have rejected the word of the Lord, he has also rejected you from being king."

Saul said: "I have sinned, for I have disobeyed the commandments of the Lord, because I feared the people and obeyed their voice. Nevertheless, pardon my sin, I pray you, and come back with me, so that I may worship the Lord."

But Samuel answered: "I will not go back with you, for you have rejected the word of the Lord, and the Lord has rejected you from being king over Israel."

Samuel turned to go away, but Saul took hold of the skirt of his mantle and the skirt tore.

Samuel said to him: "The Lord has torn the kingdom of Israel from you today, and has given it to a neighbor of yours who is better than you. The strength of Israel will not lie or repent; for he is not a man if he must repent."

Saul said: "I have done wrong, but I pray you to honor me now, before the elders of my people and before Israel, and go back with me, that I may worship the Lord your God."

Samuel relented and went back with Saul; and Saul worshiped the Lord.

Then Samuel returned to Ramah, and Saul went to his house.

As long as he lived Samuel never saw Saul again, but he mourned for him. And the Lord regretted that he had made Saul king over Israel.

DAVID THE LORD'S CHOSEN ONE

THE Lord God said to Samuel: "How long will you mourn for Saul, seeing I have rejected him from reigning over Israel? Fill your horn with oil and go. I will send you to Jesse of Bethlehem, for I have chosen a king from among his sons."

Samuel did as the Lord told him and came to Bethlehem. The elders of the town trembled at his coming and said: "Do you come peaceably?"

"Peaceably," he said, "I have come to sacrifice to the Lord. Make yourselves ready and come with me to the sacrifice."

He blessed Jesse and his sons and called them to the sacrifice.

When they came, he looked at Eliab and said: "Surely the Lord's chosen one is before him now."

But God answered, saying: "Do not look at his face or the height of him, because I have refused him. For the Lord does not see as man sees. Man looks on the outward appearance, but the Lord looks at the heart."

Then Jesse called Abinadab and made him pass before Samuel; but Samuel said: "The Lord has not chosen this one either."

Then Jesse made Shammah pass by, and Samuel said: "Neither has the Lord chosen this one."

One after the other, Jesse made seven of his sons pass before Samuel. And Samuel said to Jesse: "The Lord has not chosen these." Then he asked: "Are all your children here?"

And Jesse said: "There is still the youngest, David. He is keeping the sheep."

Samuel said to Jesse: "Send and fetch him here, for we will not sit down until he comes."

David was sent for, and soon appeared. He was a fine, healthy boy, and handsome.

Then God said to Samuel: "Arise, anoint him, for this is he."

Then Samuel took the horn of oil and anointed David in the midst of his brothers. And the Spirit of the Lord was with David from that day on.

DAVID MEETS SAUL THE KING

And the spirit of the Lord departed from Saul, and an evil spirit troubled him.

Then Saul's servants said to him: "You see, an evil spirit from God is sent to trouble you. Now if you will command your servants, who are here before you, to find a man who is a cunning player on the harp, then when the evil spirit comes from God, he will play upon the strings, and you will be well."

"Find me a man who can play well," said Saul to his servants, "and bring him to me."

Then one of the servants answered and said: "I have seen a son of Jesse the Bethlehemite, who is clever at playing, an exceedingly courageous man, a man of war, prudent in all things, a handsome person and the Lord is with him."

Therefore Saul sent messengers to

Jesse, and said: "Send me your son David, who is tending the sheep."

Jesse took an ass loaded with food, and a bottle of wine, and a kid, and sent them by David his son to Saul. And David came to Saul and stood before him, and served him.

Saul loved David very much and he was made the king's armor-bearer.

Then Saul sent word to Jesse, saying: "Let David stay with me, for he pleases me very much."

And it was true that when the evil spirit from God came upon Saul, David took a harp and played upon the strings, and Saul was refreshed and felt well again. The evil spirit departed from him at the sound of the music.

DAVID AND GOLIATH

GOLIATH CHALLENGES THE ISRAELITES

Goliath stood and cried out to the armies of Israel: "Why have you come out to set up your armies in battle array? Am I not a Philistine, and you servants of Saul? Choose a man to represent you and let him come down to me. If he can fight me and kill me, then we will be your servants, but if I win over him and kill him, then you shall be our servants and serve us." And he added: "I defy the armies of Israel this day, send me a man that we may fight together."

When Saul and all the Israelites heard those words of the Philistine, they were dismayed and very much frightened. And every morning and evening for forty days the Philistine drew near and challenged the Israelites.

David at this time left the court of Saul to go home and feed his father's sheep at Bethlehem. His three eldest brothers were in the army of Saul.

Now Jesse said to David his son: "Take a measure of this parched grain and these ten loaves for your brothers and run to your brothers' camp. Take these ten cheeses to the captain of their group, and see how your brothers are faring."

David rose early in the morning and left the sheep with a keeper, and departed as Jesse had commanded him. He came to the battle line just as the army was going out to fight, shouting their battle cry. For Israel and the Philistines had put the army in battle array, army against army.

David left his baggage in the hands of the keeper of the baggage, and ran among the army. He came up to his brothers and saluted them.

As he talked with them, there appeared the champion Goliath, out of the armies of the Philistines, and he made his challenge, and David heard it.

OW the Philistines gathered their forces for battle. They gathered at Shochoh, and they camped in Ephes-dammim.

Saul and the men of Israel were gathered together and camped in the valley of Elah, lined up in battle array against the Philistines.

The Philistines stood on a mountain on one side, and Israel stood on a mountain on the other side, and there was a valley between them.

Out from the camp of the Philistines came a champion named Goliath of Gath, whose height was nine feet and nine inches. He had a helmet of brass upon his head, and he was armed with a coat of mail, and the weight of the coat was five thousand shekels of brass. He had plates of brass upon his legs, and a shield of brass between his shoulders. The staff of his spear was like a weaver's beam, and his spear's head weighed six hundred shekels of iron. A shield bearer walked before him.

All the men of Israel, when they saw the man, fled from him and were very much afraid. "Have you seen this man who came up?" the men of Israel said. "He has come up to challenge Israel, and to the man who can kill him the king will give great riches, and he will give him his daughter in marriage, and will make his father's house free in Israel."

And David spoke to the men who stood near him, saying: "Who is this heathen Philistine, that he should chal-

and the wickedness of your heart, for you have come down just so that you might see the battle."

David said: "What have I now done? Is there not a reason?" He turned from him toward another man and spoke to him in the same way, and the people spoke again of the reward.

And when the people heard the words which David spoke, they repeated them before Saul, and he sent for the boy.

lenge the armies of the living God?"

Eliab, his eldest brother, heard him speak to the men, and Eliab's anger was kindled against David, and he said: "Why did you come down here? With whom did you leave those few sheep in the wilderness? I know your pride

DAVID OFFERS TO FIGHT

And David said to Saul: "Let no man's heart be troubled because of Goliath. I, your servant, will go and fight with this Philistine."

Saul said: "You are not able to go

out to fight with this Philistine, for you are but a boy, and he has been a man of war since his youth."

David said to Saul: "Your servant kept his father's sheep, and a lion came, and a bear, and took a lamb out of the flock. I gave chase, and struck the lion down, and rescued it out of his mouth, and when he arose against me, I caught him by his beard and struck him and killed him. Your servant killed both the lion and the bear, and this heathen Philistine will be as one

Then Saul said to David: "Go, and the Lord be with you."

Saul armed David with his armor, and he put a helmet of brass on his head, and clothed him in a coat of mail. David fastened Saul's sword upon his armor and tried to walk, in order to test the armor, but finding he could not, he said to Saul: "I cannot fight with these, for I am not used to them." Saul's pieces of armor were too heavy and cumbersome so he undid them and took them off.

of them, seeing that he has challenged the armies of the living God."

Moreover, David said: "The Lord who saved me from the paw of the lion and from the paw of the bear, he will save me from the hand of this Philistine."

He took his staff in his hand, and bending down chose five smooth stones out of the brook, and put them in a shepherd's bag which he carried with him. With his sling in his hand he drew near to the giant Philistine, who waited.

TRIUMPH WITH A SLING

The Philistine came on and drew near to David, and the shield bearer went before him. But when the Philistine looked and saw David, he despised him, for he was but a boy, fine and fair of face.

The Philistine said to David: "Am I a dog, that you come to fight me with sticks?" And the Philistine cursed David by his gods.

And the Philistine said to David: "Come to me, and I will give your flesh to the fowls of the air, and to the beasts of the field."

Then David said to the Philistine: "You come to me with a sword and with a spear and with a shield, but I come to you in the name of the Lord of hosts, the God of the army of Israel, whom you have challenged. This day the Lord will put you into my hands, and I will strike you down and take your head from you, and I will give the bodies of the army of the Philistines to the birds of the air and to the wild beasts of the earth, so that all the earth may know that there is a God in Israel. And everyone gathered here will know that the Lord saves not with sword and spear, but the battle is the Lord's and he will give you into our hands."

Then, as the Philistine rose up and came nearer to meet David, David hurried and ran toward the army to meet the Philistine. And he put his hand into his bag, and took out a stone, and slung it, and hit the Philistine in his forehead, so that the stone sank into his forehead and he fell upon his face on the earth.

So David triumphed over the Philistine with a sling and with a stone, and struck down the Philistine and killed him; but there was no sword in David's hand.

Therefore David ran and stood upon the Philistine and taking Goliath's sword cut off his head and killed him.

When the Philistines saw that their champion was dead, they fled. And the men of Israel arose, shouting, and pursued the Philistines all the way to the valley, to the gates of Ekron.

The Philistines who were wounded fell down by the road to Shaaraim, as far as Gath and Ekron. Then the children of Israel came back from chasing the Philistines and pillaged their tents. And David took the head of the Philistine and brought it to Jerusalem; but he put the armor in his own tent.

And when Saul had seen David going forth against Goliath, he had said to Abner, his general: "Abner, whose son is this youth?

Abner said: "Upon my word, O king, I do not know."

The king said: "Find out who is this stripling's father."

And as David returned from the slaughter of the Philistine, Abner took him and brought him before Saul with Goliath's head in his hand.

And Saul said: "Whose son are you, young man?"

David said: "I am the son of your servant, Jesse the Bethlehemite."

SAUL'S JEALOUSY

SAUL took David home that day, and would not let him go back to his father's house. He set him over all his men of war, and the people and the palace servants accepted him. Jonathan, Saul's son, came to love David as his own brother, and they made a covenant of friendship.

But as David was returning from the slaughter of the Philistines, the women came out of the cities of Israel, singing and dancing, to meet king Saul, with tabrets and other musical instruments. And the women sang to each other as they played, and said:

"Saul has slain his thousands,
And David his ten thousands."

This much displeased Saul, and he said: "If they reckon that David is ten times better than I, he will soon want to have the kingdom for himself."

And from this time forward Saul eyed David with suspicion.

The next day, David was playing his harp as before, and an evil spirit came upon Saul and he picked up a javelin and threw it at David, saying: "I will pin David to the wall with it."

David avoided the point of the javelin, and Saul was more than ever afraid of him, for he knew that the Lord was with David, and no longer with him.

But David behaved very wisely in all his ways and all Israel loved and trusted him.

Then Saul said to David: "Here is my elder daughter Merab. I will give her to you as your wife, if you will fight my battles for me." For Saul did not want to kill David with his own hand, and he hoped that he would fall in battle with the Philistines.

David said: "Who am I, and what is my family, that I should be the king's son-in-law?"

But at the time that Merab should have been given to David, instead Saul married her to Adriel the Meholathite.

But it happened that Michal, Saul's younger daughter, also loved David, and when Saul was told of this, he was very pleased, thinking that through her love he might ensnare and destroy David.

So he sent for David and told him: "Today you will be my son-in-law, and marry the other of my daughters."

To his servants he said: "Take David aside and tell him privately that the king delights in him, and that all the people love him, and so it is fitting that he should be the king's son-in-law."

DAVID MARRIES SAUL'S DAUGHTER

But when he heard this, David said: "I am too poor and insignificant to marry a king's daughter."

The servants reported this to Saul and he said: "Tell David that the king does not wish for any dowry, only the death of a hundred Philistines, to be avenged of the king's enemies."

When David heard this he was pleased, for he wanted very much to be the king's son-in-law, so he went forth with his men and slew two hundred Philistines, and Saul gave him Michal as his wife.

But Saul saw and knew that the Lord was with David, and that Michal loved him, and he was still more afraid of David, and still more his enemy.

And Saul spoke to Jonathan his son and to all his servants and ordered them to kill David. But Jonathan went to his friend and said: "My father Saul is trying to kill you, so I beg of you to go and hide yourself. Tomorrow morning I shall go out and stand beside my father in the field where you are, and I will talk to him about you, and whatever I learn I shall tell you."

The next day Jonathan talked to Saul as he had promised, and told him what a great and good man David was, and urged his father not to stain his hands with innocent blood.

Saul listened to Jonathan's words and promised that David should not be slain.

So Jonathan called David from his hiding place and brought him before Saul and for a time all was well, and when the Philistines went to war again, David fought against them and slew many of them.

But again Saul was possessed by an evil spirit, and sat with his javelin in his hand while David played the harp. Again he tried to kill David, and again

David slipped out of the path of the javelin and escaped from the palace.

Saul sent messengers to his house to watch and slay him in the morning, and Michal, David's wife, said to her husband: "If you do not get away tonight, tomorrow you will be killed."

So Michal let David down through a window, and then she made up the bed to look as though David were lying asleep in it.

And when Saul sent his messengers to take David, she said: "He is ill."

But Saul sent the messengers back to see David, saying: "Bring him up to me in his bed and I shall slay him."

When the messengers came in, they saw that there was no one in the bed.

Saul said to Michal: "Why have you deceived me and helped my enemy to escape."

Michal answered: "He said to me, 'Let me escape; otherwise I shall kill you.'"

When David fled he took refuge with Samuel at Naioth in Ramah.

DAVID
AND
JONATHAN

AVID left Naioth and came to Jonathan and said to him: "What have I done that your father should try to kill me?"

Jonathan said: "I will do all in my power to try to save you. I know that my father will do nothing without consulting me, so I shall speak to him about your fate and tell you what he says. If he is ill disposed toward you, I shall warn you so that you may flee, but whatever passes, we shall remain friends for ever and ever."

So they made a solemn covenant of friendship, for Jonathan loved David as he loved his own soul.

Then Jonathan said to David: "Tomorrow is the feast of the new moon, and you will be missed, because your seat will be empty. When you have stayed away three days, come down quickly and wait by the stone Ezel. I will shoot three arrows beside the stone, as if I shot at a target. And watch, I will send a boy, saying: 'Go, find the arrows.' If I expressly say to the boy, 'See the arrows are on this side of you, pick them up,' then you come out, for there will be peace and no harm will be done to you, as the Lord lives. But if I say to the young man, 'See, the arrows are beyond you,' go your way, for the Lord will have sent you away. And

concerning friendship of which we have spoken, may the Lord be between you and me for ever."

So David hid himself in the field.

When the moon had come, the king sat down to the feast. The king sat upon his seat, as always, a seat along the wall, and Jonathan and Abner sat beside Saul, but David's place was empty.

Still Saul did not say anything that day.

But it happened on the next day, which was the second day of the month, that David's place was empty again, and Saul said to Jonathan: "Why did the son of Jesse not come to dinner either yesterday or today?"

And Jonathan answered: "David earnestly asked permission of me to go to Bethlehem, for he said his family was to have a sacrifice there, and his brother had bidden him to come, and he desired to see all his brothers. That is why he did not come to the king's table."

Then Saul's anger was kindled against Jonathan, and he said to him: "You son of a perverse, rebellious woman, do I not know that you have chosen the son of Jesse to your own downfall? For as long as he lives, you shall not be established in the kingdom. Now send and fetch him to me, for he must die."

But Jonathan answered Saul his father, and said to him: "Why should he be slain? What has he done?"

Then Saul threw a javelin at him to strike him, and by that Jonathan knew that his father was determined to kill David. So Jonathan arose from the table in fierce anger, and ate not at all the second day of the month, for he grieved for David.

In the morning Jonathan went out into the field at the time he had set with David, taking a little boy with him.

He said to the lad: "Run and hunt for the arrows which I am going to shoot." And as the lad ran, he shot an arrow beyond him.

When the lad had come to the place where the arrow fell, Jonathan cried out to the lad and said: "Is not the arrow beyond you?" And again he cried: "Make haste, do not delay!"

Jonathan's lad took up the fallen arrow and came to his master, but the lad did not understand the meaning.

Only Jonathan and David knew of the matter.

Then Jonathan gave his weapons to the lad, and said to him: "Go, carry them down to the city." And as soon as the lad was gone, David rose up from a place toward the south and fell on his face on the ground, and bowed himself three times.

They kissed each other and wept with each other, and Jonathan said to David: "Go in peace, for we have both sworn in the name of the Lord, saying, 'May the Lord be between you and me, and between your children and my children for ever.' "

David arose and departed, and Jonathan went back to the city.

SAUL'S WRATH

AVID came to Ahimelech, the priest of Nob. He asked for food and Ahimelech gave him some of the hallowed bread. Because he had no weapons, Ahimelech brought out the sword of Goliath which lay wrapped in a cloth, and said: "If you want this sword, it is yours, for it is the only one here."

So David took the sword of Goliath, the Philistine whom he had slain, but as he was afraid of the wrath of Saul, he went and hid in the cave of Adullam. When his brothers and all his father's house heard that he was there, they came to him. And everyone that was in distress, and everyone that was in debt, and everyone that was discontented, gathered themselves unto him. He became a captain over them and there were about four hundred men with him.

One of the foremost herdsmen of Saul, Doeg the Edomite, was at Nob when David visited the priest Ahimelech. He came to Saul and told him how the priest gave unto David food and a sword. When he heard this, Saul sent to Nob and commanded Ahimelech and all his family to come before him.

When they came to him, Saul said: "Why have you conspired against me with the son of Jesse, and given him bread and a sword? And why did you intercede with the Lord for him and against me?"

Ahimelech answered: "You have no more faithful subject than David. Is he not your son-in-law, obedient to your bidding and honored in your house? Did I intercede with the Lord for

him? Never. Let not the king impute such a thing to his servant nor to all the house of my father, for your servant knew nothing about this matter and pleads his innocence."

The king said: "You shall surely die, Ahimelech, you and all your father's house." And he said to the soldiers who stood beside him: "Kill the priests of the Lord, for they are friends of David, and they knew when he fled and did not tell me."

But the servants of the king would not slay the priests of the Lord.

So the king said to Doeg the Edomite: "Fall upon the priests of the Lord. They are enemies to me."

Doeg the Edomite turned and fell upon the priests, and on that day he slew eighty-five of them. And he attacked the city of Nob and killed everything inside it.

Only one of the sons of Ahimelech,

named Abiathar, escaped and fled to David. He told David that Saul had killed the Lord's priests.

David said: "I knew it that day, that Doeg the Edomite would certainly tell Saul, so I am responsible for the death of all the members of your father's house. You must stay with me, and do not be afraid, for he who threatens my life, threatens your life, but with me you will be well guarded and protected."

DAVID
AND
ABIGAIL

AMUEL died and all the Israelites were gathered together to lament him, and they buried him in his house at Ramah. And David arose and went down to the wilderness of Paran.

There was a man in Maon who owned land in Carmel. His name was Nabal, of the house of Caleb, and he was very rich. He had three thousand goats and a thousand sheep and his sheep were being shorn in Carmel. His wife was called Abigail and she was wise and beautiful, but Nabal was churlish and evil in his doings.

In the wilderness David heard that Nabal was shearing his sheep, so he called out ten of his young men and said to them: "Go to Carmel and greet Nabal from me, and say to him, 'Peace be to you and your house and all that you have. We have not harmed your shepherds while they were shearing near us in Carmel, nor have we stolen anything. So find favor with these young men, and pray give unto them, for themselves and for your son David.'"

The young men came and repeated this to Nabal, but he answered: "Who is David? And who is the son of Jesse? Many servants break away from

their masters nowadays, and shall I take my bread and water, and the meat that I have killed for my shearers, and give it to these men of whom I know nothing?"

The young men went back to David, and told him how they had fared, and David said: "Gird on your swords." He also girded on his sword, and four hundred men went with David, leaving two hundred behind to look after their goods.

But one of Nabal's young men told Abigail about this, saying: "David sent messengers out of the wilderness to salute our master, but he insulted them. But they were very good to us, nothing was stolen and nobody was hurt, and they were like our defenders

during the time that we were together in the fields. What can we do now, for they are marching against our master, but he is such an evil man that nobody can speak to him."

Then Abigail made haste and took two hundred loaves and two bottles of wine and five sheep already cooked, and five measures of parched corn, and a hundred bunches of raisins and two hundred cakes of figs, and loaded them on asses. And she said to her servants: "Go on ahead of me and I shall follow." But she said nothing of this to her husband.

As she rode on the ass, she met David and his men and she alighted from her ass and fell at David's feet and bowed to the ground before him and said: "Listen, I beseech you, to the words of your handmaid. Pay no heed to this Nabal, this son of Belial, for he is a fool. I did not see the young men whom you sent, but I beg of you not to shed blood nor to avenge yourself upon your enemy. For the Lord will fight your battles even as you fight the battles of the Lord. And in the day of your triumph I implore you to remember your handmaid."

David said to Abigail: "Blessed be the Lord God of Israel for sending you here, and blessed be your counsel. Had you not come, I would surely have slain Nabal and all his household." Then he accepted her gifts and said: "Go in peace to your own house, for I will heed your advice."

Abigail went back to Nabal, who was holding a feast. He was drunk, so she told him nothing of what had happened. But the next morning, when he was sober, she told him, and Nabal's heart fainted within him, and he became as stone. And it came to pass that about ten days later, the Lord smote Nabal and he died.

When David heard that Nabal was dead, he praised God and sent for Abigail, intending to marry her, for Saul had given David's wife Michal in marriage to Phalti, the son of Laish.

When Abigail heard that David wished to marry her, she bowed her face to the ground and said: "Let me be a handmaid to wash the feet of the servants of my lord."

Then she mounted an ass, taking five young girls with her, and went with the messengers of David, and became his wife.

stole away, and no man saw him or knew that he was there or waked up, for they were all asleep. A deep sleep from the Lord had fallen upon them.

Then David went and stood on the top of a hill far off, a long distance from the camp.

David cried to the people, and to Abner, saying: "Are you not a courageous man? Who is like you in Israel? Why then have you not protected the lord your king? For one of the people came to destroy the king your lord. Look now for the king's spear and the jug of water that was beside his pillow."

Then Saul knew David's voice and said: "Is that your voice, my son David?"

And David said: "It is my voice, my lord, O king." And he added: "Why does my lord pursue his serv-

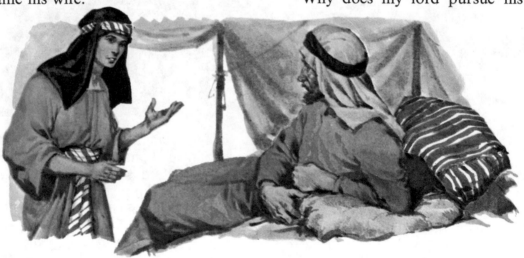

DAVID SPARES SAUL'S LIFE

David arose one night and came to where Saul had set up his tent. David saw the place where Saul lay, and Abner, the son of Ner, the captain of his army, lay beside him. Saul lay in the middle of the camp, and his men were encamped around him.

So David took the spear and the jug of water from beside Saul's pillow, and

ant this way? What have I done? What is the evil within me?"

Then Saul said: "I have sinned. Return to me, my son David, for I will never more do you any harm, because my life was precious to you this day. I see now that I have been foolish and very wrong."

Then Saul blessed David. And David went on his way, and Saul returned to the palace.

SAUL AND THE SPIRIT OF SAMUEL

OW the Philistines gathered themselves together and came and pitched in Shunem. Then Saul gathered all Israel together and they pitched in Gilboa. And when Saul saw the army of the Philistines, he was afraid and his heart trembled greatly. But when Saul questioned the Lord, the Lord answered him not.

Then Saul said to his servants: "Seek me a woman that is a medium, that I may go to her and inquire of her." And his servants said: "There is a woman that is a medium at Endor." So Saul disguised himself and came to the woman by night. He said to her: "I pray you, bring forth the spirit whose name I shall give you."

Then the woman said: "Whom shall I bring up to you?" And he said: "Bring me up Samuel." And when the woman saw Samuel, she cried with a loud voice and spoke to Saul, saying: "Why have you deceived me? For you are Saul."

The king said to her: "Be not afraid. What did you see? What is he like?" She said: "An old man, and he is covered with a robe." And Saul knew that it was Samuel, and he stooped with his face to the ground, and bowed himself.

And Samuel said to Saul: "Why have you disturbed me?" Saul said: "I am greatly distressed, for the Philistines make war against me, and God has departed from me, and no longer answers me. Therefore I have called you, that you may make known to me what I shall do."

Then Samuel said: "Why do you ask me, seeing that the Lord has departed from you, and has become your enemy? The Lord has done to you as he spoke by me: he has broken up your kingdom and given it to your neighbor, to David. Moreover, the Lord will also deliver Israel with you into the hand of the Philistines,

and tomorrow you and your sons shall be with me."

Then Saul fell flat on the earth and was much afraid because of the words of Samuel, and there was no strength in him, for he had eaten no bread all day nor all night.

The woman saw that he was troubled and said to him: "Let me set a morsel of bread before you, and eat, that you may have strength when you go on your way." But he refused and said: "I will not eat."

Then his servants, together with the woman, compelled him to eat. He arose from the earth and sat upon a bed. Saul and his servants ate. Then they rose up, gathered their things, and went away in the night.

SAUL KILLS HIMSELF

Now the Philistines fought against Israel and the men of Israel fled from before the Philistines and were slain by them on Mount Gilboa. And the Philistines followed closely after Saul and his sons, and Saul himself was hard pressed in the battle and severely wounded by the Philistine archers.

Then Saul said to his armor-bearer: "Draw your sword and run me through with it, lest these heathen kill me and then dishonor my body."

But his armor-bearer dared not do such a thing.

Therefore Saul took a sword and fell upon it, and when the armor-bearer saw that Saul was dead, he also fell

upon his sword and died with his king.

So Saul perished with his three sons and his armor-bearer, and all his men, on that same day together.

And when the men of Israel, who were on the other side of the valley and the other side of Jordan, saw that Saul and his sons were dead and his army defeated, they forsook the cities and fled. And the Philistines came and dwelt in them.

Lest the daughters of the uncircumcised
  triumph.
Ye mountains of Gilboa, let there be no dew.
Neither let there be rain upon you,
  nor fields of offerings;
For there the shield of the mighty
  is vilely cast away,
The shield of Saul, as though he
  had not been anointed with oil.
From the blood of the slain,
  from the fat of the mighty,
The bow of Jonathan turned not back,
And the sword of Saul returned not empty.
Saul and Jonathan were lovely
  and pleasant in their lives,
And in their death they were not divided.
They were swifter than eagles,
They were stronger than lions.
Ye daughters of Israel, weep over Saul,
Who clothed you in scarlet,
  with other delights,
Who put on ornaments of gold upon your
  apparel.
How are the mighty fallen in the midst
  of the battle!
O Jonathan, thou wast slain
  in thine high places.
I am distressed for thee,
  my brother Jonathan,
Very pleasant hast thou been unto me.
Thy love to me was wonderful,
  passing the love of women.
How are the mighty fallen,
  and the weapons of war perished!

DAVID'S LAMENT FOR SAUL AND JONATHAN

When David learned of the death of Saul and Jonathan, he tore his clothes and fasted, and so did all the men who were with him. They mourned and wept and fasted until the evening, for Saul and for Israel; because they had fallen by the sword.

And David lamented with this lamentation over Saul and over Jonathan his son.

The beauty of Israel is slain upon
  thy high places:
How are the mighty fallen!
Tell it not in Gath,
Publish it not in the streets of Askelon,
Lest the daughters of the Philistines rejoice,

And it came to pass after this that the Lord told David to go up to Hebron. So he took his people, every man with his household and he led them across the plain and into the city. There they anointed him king over the house of Judah.

But Abner, the son of Ner, captain of Saul's army, took Ishbosheth, the son of Saul, and brought him to Mahanaim, and made him king over Gilead, and over the Ashurites, and over all Israel. Ishbosheth was forty years old when he began to reign over Israel, and reigned two years. But David and the house of Judah were stronger than they.

DAVID
THE KING

AND it came to pass that, after the death of Abner and Ishbosheth, all the tribes of Israel came to David in Hebron and spoke saying: "Behold, we are your bone and your flesh. Also, in time past, when Saul was king over us, you were our leader in Israel, and the Lord said to you: 'You shall feed my people Israel and you shall be a captain over Israel.'"

So king David made a league with them in Hebron before the Lord, and they anointed David king over Israel. David was thirty years old when he began to reign, and he reigned forty years. In Hebron he reigned over Judah seven years and six months, and in Jerusalem he reigned thirty and three years over all Israel and Judah.

DAVID CAPTURES JERUSALEM

David and his men went to Jerusalem, to the Jebusites, the inhabitants of the land, who spoke to him, saying: "Except that you take away the blind and the lame, you shall not come in here." Nevertheless, David encircled and overtook the stronghold of Zion.

He dwelt in the fort, and called it the city of David. And he built round about from Millo and inward. And David went on, and grew great, and the Lord God of hosts was with him.

THE HOUSE OF JUDAH SPREADS

After this it came to pass that David smote the Philistines and subdued them. And he smote Moab, and the Moabites became David's servants, and brought gifts. David smote also Hadadezer, the son of Rehob, king of Zobah, as he went to regain his border at the river Euphrates.

David took from him a thousand chariots and seven hundred horsemen and twenty thousand footmen. And when the Syrians of Damascus came to help Hadadezer, David slew twenty-two thousand of the Syrians. David put garrisons in Syria and the Syrians became David's servants and brought gifts. And the Lord preserved David wherever he went.

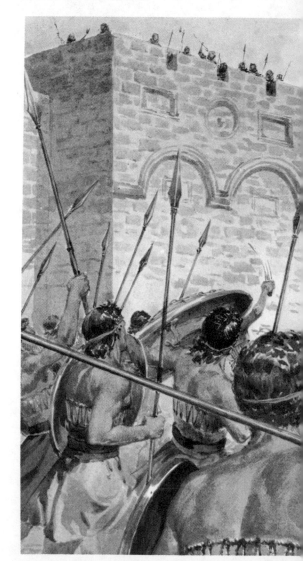

DAVID FINDS JONATHAN'S SON

But after all his victories David said, "Is there any that is left of the house of Saul, that I may show him kindness for Jonathan's sake?" A servant of the house of Saul whose name was Ziba was called unto David. And the king asked him, "Is there not any still of the house of Saul that I may show kindness unto him?" And Ziba said unto the king, "Jonathan has a son who is lame on his feet." So the king gave orders to fetch the son.

Now when the son of Jonathan, whose name was Mephibosheth, had come unto David, he fell on his face and did reverence. And David said, "Mephibosheth!" And he answered, "Behold your servant!" David said unto him, "Fear not: for I will show you kindness for Jonathan, your father's sake and I will restore to you all the lands of Saul your grandfather; and you shall eat with me at my table continually." And Mephibosheth said, "Why should you be so kind unto such a dead dog as I am?"

Then the king called to Ziba, and said unto him, "I have given to your master's grandson all that belonged to Saul. You and your sons, and your servants, shall till the land for him, and shall bring in fruits that your master's son may have food to eat: but Mephibosheth your master's son shall eat bread always at my table." So Mephibosheth dwelt in Jerusalem and dined always at David's table and was lame on both his feet.

DAVID AND BATHSHEBA

 T was the time when kings go forth to battle, and David sent Joab, his general, and his servants with him, and they destroyed the children of Ammon and besieged Rabbah. But David remained in Jerusalem.

One evening he rose from his bed and walked on the roof of his palace. He saw a very beautiful woman and sent to ask who she was. He was told: "She is Bathsheba, the daughter of Eliam, the wife of Uriah the Hittite."

David fell in love with Bathsheba, and he sent to Joab, saying: "Send me Uriah the Hittite."

So Joab sent Uriah to David, and when he came the king asked how Joab and the army were, and how the war prospered. Then he gave Uriah food and told him he could go to his own home. But Uriah slept at the door of the king's house with all the servants of his lord.

The next morning David asked him why he had not gone to his own home, and Uriah answered: "The ark and Israel and Judah live in tents, and my lord Joab and the servants of my lord are encamped in the open fields. Shall I go home to my wife to eat and drink and sleep in comfort? As the Lord lives, and as your soul lives, I cannot do such a thing."

David said: "Wait until tomorrow and I shall let you go back."

Then David wrote a letter to Joab and sent it to him by the hand of Uriah. In it he said: "Set Uriah in the forefront of the hottest battle, and withdraw from him, so that he may be smitten and die."

When Joab was besieging the city, he assigned Uriah to a place where the bravest defenders were. The men of the city came out and fought with Joab, and some of his soldiers were killed, and among them was Uriah the Hittite.

When Bathsheba learned that Uriah was dead she wept for him. But when the days of her mourning were past, David sent and fetched her to his house, and she became his wife and bore him a son.

But the thing that David had done displeased the Lord. And the Lord sent Nathan to David.

DAVID JUDGES HIMSELF

Nathan came and said to him: "There were two men in one city, one rich and the other poor. The rich man had many flocks and herds, but the poor man had nothing except one little ewe lamb which he had bought and reared, so that it grew up with him and his children. It ate from his hand and drank from his cup, and he carried it in his arms, and it was like a daughter to him. And a traveler came to the rich man and asked for a meal. His host spared his own flocks and herds, but he took the poor man's lamb and killed and cooked it for the wayfarer."

When David heard this he was very angry, and he said to Nathan: "As the Lord lives, the man that has done this thing must surely die. And he must refund the value of the lamb four times over, because he did this thing and had no pity."

And Nathan said to David: "You are the man! The Lord God of Israel has given you so much, why have you disregarded the commandment of the Lord and done evil in his sight? You killed Uriah the Hittite with the sword of the children of Ammon and took his wife to be your wife."

David said to Nathan: "I have sinned before the Lord."

Nathan said: "The Lord has forgiven you your sin, and you shall not die. But because this deed has given rise to talk among the enemies of the Lord, the child that has been born to you will surely die."

Having said this, Nathan went back to his own home.

The child of Bathsheba and David fell sick, and David prayed to God, and fasted, and lay all night on the ground. He would neither eat nor drink, but on the seventh day the child died.

The servants of David were afraid to tell him that the child was dead, for they said: "While the child was still alive he would not listen when we spoke to him, so how will he be when we tell him that it is dead?"

But David saw that his servants were whispering together, and he knew that the child was dead. He asked them if it was so, and they said: "He is dead."

Then David arose and washed and anointed himself, and changed his clothes and came into the house of the Lord and worshiped. Then he went into his own house and when he required, they set bread before him and he sat down to eat.

His servants asked him: "How is it that you fasted and wept for the child while it was alive, and now that it is dead, you get up and eat again?"

He said: "While the child was still alive, I fasted and wept, for I thought 'Who can tell whether God will be gracious unto me, and allow the child to live?' But now that he is dead, why should I go on fasting? Can I bring him back again? I shall go to him, but he cannot return to me."

Then David consoled Bathsheba his wife, and in due course they had another son whom they called Solomon, and the Lord loved him.

DAVID AND ABSALOM

IN all Israel there was no handsomer man than Absalom, the king's favorite son. From the sole of his foot to the crown of his head, there was no blemish in him. He cut his hair every year when it became too heavy for his head, and his hair weighed two hundred shekels on the king's scales.

And king David loved Absalom very dearly.

Absalom had chariots and horses and fifty men to attend him. He would rise early in the morning and wait at the gate near the place of judgment, and if anybody came with a case to lay before the king, Absalom would call unto him and ask where he came from. If the man said that he was an Israelite, Absalom would say: "You are certainly in the right, but there is nobody here to represent you. If I were judge, any man could come to me with his cause and I would do him justice."

If any man came to bow down to Absalom he would have none of it, but took him by the hand and kissed him. And so Absalom stole the hearts of the men of Israel.

One day he said to the king: "Let me go to Hebron to fulfill a vow which I made to the Lord while I was in Syria."

King David said: "Go in peace."

So Absalom went to Hebron, and he sent spies throughout all the tribes of Israel, saying: "As soon as you hear the sound of a trumpet, then you must proclaim that Absalom rules in Hebron."

Absalom had with him two hundred men from Jerusalem who knew nothing of the conspiracy, and more and more people turned to Absalom.

Then a messenger came to David and warned him and he said to all his servants: "We must flee, or otherwise we shall not be able to escape from Absalom." So he fled from Jerusalem with all his household, but the ark of the Lord and Zadok the priest remained in the city.

So there was war between David and his son Absalom. David divided his army in three parts and he was prepared to go forth with it, but his people said: "You must not go forth, for nobody cares about us except you. You are worth ten thousand of us, so it is better that you should lead us from inside the city."

David said: "I will do whatever you think best."

He stood by the gate and the people came out by the hundreds and thousands. He spoke to his commanders, Joab and Abishai and Ittai, and said: "Deal gently, for my sake, with the young man, Absalom." And all the people heard what he said about Absalom.

A great battle was fought in the wood of Ephraim, and the people of Israel were defeated by the armies of David, and twenty thousand men were killed.

ABSALOM IS KILLED

Absalom met the servants of David. He was riding a horse, and the horse went under a great oak, and Absalom's head was caught up in the thick boughs of the oak, so that he dangled between heaven and earth, and his horse galloped away from beneath him. A man saw him there and told Joab, saying: "I have seen Absalom, hanging in an oak."

Joab said: "Since you saw him why did you not strike him to the ground? I would have given you ten shekels of silver."

The man said: "Not for a thousand shekels of silver would I raise my hand against the king's son, for I heard the king telling you and Abishai and Ittai not to touch the young man Absalom. It would have been as much as my life was worth, for nothing can be hidden from the king, and you yourself would have blamed me."

"I cannot tarry thus with you," said Joab. He took three darts in his hand and thrust them into the heart of Absalom, who was still alive and hanging from the oak. And ten of Joab's young men surrounded Absalom and stabbed him to death.

DAVID RECEIVES THE NEWS

David sat between the two gates and the watchman went up to the roof over the gate by the wall, and saw a man running toward the city. The watchman told the king, and the king said: "If he is alone, he must be coming with news."

Then the watchman saw another man and he said to the king: "The first man runs very like Ahimaaz the son of Zadok."

The king said: "He is a good man, he will be coming with good news."

Ahimaaz called up to the king and said: "All is well."

Then he fell on his face before the king and said: "Blessed be the Lord God which has delivered up the men who lifted their hand against my lord the king."

The king said: "Is the young man Absalom safe?"

Ahimaaz said: "When Joab sent me

and the other messenger, everything was in great confusion, and I do not know what was happening."

The king said: "Go, and stand aside."

Then the other messenger, Cushi, arrived, and he said: "News, my lord king. The Lord has avenged you on those who rebelled against you."

And the king said to Cushi: "Is the young man Absalom safe?"

Cushi said: "May the enemies of my lord the king and all that seek to harm you, be as Absalom is now!"

The king was greatly distressed, and he went up to the chamber over the gate, weeping and saying: "O my son Absalom, my son, my son Absalom. Would God I had died for you, O Absalom, my son, my son!"

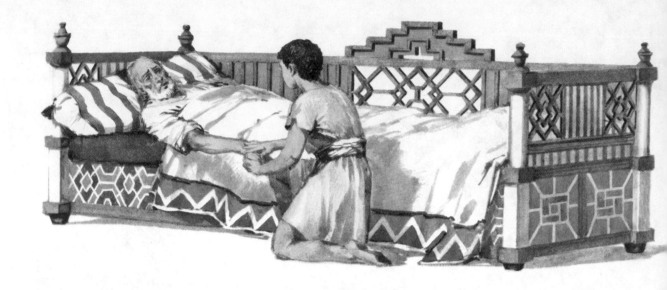

THE DEATH OF DAVID

 OW King David was old and stricken in years; they wrapped him in clothes but he lost strength daily. The end of his life drew near and he knew that he must die.

He sent for his son Solomon and charged him, saying: "I go the way of all the earth; therefore you must be strong and show yourself to be a man. Keep the commandments of the Lord your God and walk in his ways. Obey his statutes and abide by his word as it is written in the law of Moses. Then the Lord will fulfill his promises that he made to me saying: 'If thy children take heed to their way, to walk before me in truth with all their heart and all their soul, there shall always be male children for the throne of Israel.' You know what I have endured. Be wise therefore in all that you do."

And in his last words to the people, David spoke of the qualities of kingship in these words: "The God of Israel spoke to me saying:

'He that ruleth over men must be just, ruling in the fear of God. And he shall be as the light of the morning when the sun rises, as a morning without clouds; as tender grass, springing out of the earth, in clear sunshine after rain.'"

So David slept with his fathers and was buried in the city of David, after reigning over Israel for forty years: seven years in Hebron and thirty-three years in Jerusalem.

And Solomon sat on the throne of David his father, and ruled over his kingdom.

ILLUSTRATED
GLOSSARY

Armor (p. 349)

Clothing made of heavy material, such as leather or metal, that is worn as a protection from battle injuries is called armor. Saul's armor was a helmet and a coat of mail. (See Coat of mail.) It was probably made of bronze or copper. The Philistines also wore greaves, metal coverings for their lower legs, and were well supplied with armor because they had a good metal industry.

At this time only kings and other leaders were equipped with armor. It wasn't until much later that common soldiers had armor.

Armor-bearer (p. 345)

A man or boy acted as an armor-bearer for a soldier by carrying shields, javelins, and helmets that were not in use at the moment.

Benjamite (p. 336)

A Benjamite was from the tribe of Benjamin. King Saul was a Benjamite.

Bribes and false judgments (p. 336)

Samuel's sons were dishonest men who took gifts (bribes) in return for granting favors or overlooking the law (delivering false judgments) to benefit the gift-giver.

"By your thousands" (p. 340)

Since the days of Jacob, the Hebrews had been divided into tribes. By the time of the exodus, however, the tribes had grown very large and were subdivided into groups of one thousand people each. This made administration much easier. When Samuel said the Israelites were to present themselves by their tribes and by their thousands, he meant these groups of a thousand people.

Coat of mail (p. 346)

A coat of mail was a garment like a long shirt that was made of heavy cloth or leather and was covered with small metal plates. The metal helped protect its wearer from swords and javelins. The Israelites wore coats of mail that reached to the knees. Other peoples sometimes wore coats of mail that reached to the ankles.

"Cursed be the man that eats any food until evening" (p. 341)

Saul was telling his people to fast (see Fast) as a way of showing respect for God so that God would help him defeat the Philistines. Saul wanted revenge on the nation that had consistently defeated the Israelites. He threatened to call down a curse, an evil spell, on those who disobeyed.

Dowry (p. 354)

A dowry was money paid to the father of a bridegroom by the bride's father or family. Upon payment of the dowry the young people were considered legally married. However, a lavish wedding followed some time later. During biblical times, marriages were frequently arranged by the parents, and the bride and groom often met each other for the first time at their wedding.

Fallen by the sword (p. 367)

To fall by the sword usually means to die in battle. When David wept because Saul and Israel had fallen by the sword, this meant that Saul was dead, and that Israel had been defeated in battle.

Fast (p. 367)

The Hebrews ate no food, and usually went without water, as a way of dedicating their bodies to God. Israelite soldiers often performed the difficult deed of fasting before a battle to show God they were putting themselves completely in his hands.

Feast of the new moon (p. 356)

Each time a new moon was seen in the sky a feast was celebrated. On that evening a new month began. Celebrations of the new moons were later remembered in the New Moon Sabbaths.

"Fill your horn" (p. 344)

God was telling Samuel to fill an animal's horn, probably the horn of an ox, with olive oil. He would need the oil to anoint the person God had chosen to be the next king.

Footmen (p. 335)

Footmen were ordinary soldiers, fighting men who went to battle on foot and fought on foot. Other soldiers were chariot soldiers, who went to battle in chariots, and cavalry men who rode to battle on mounts.

Hallowed bread (p. 358)

Hallowed bread, also called showbread, was placed on the altar as an offering to God. It was made holy because it had been set before the Lord.

Although only priests were allowed to eat this bread, it was given to David because he was hungry and the priest had no other bread.

Harp (p. 344)

Harps are stringed musical instruments that are usually plucked with the fingers. The harps of biblical times were much smaller than those we use today, and could be carried about or held on the lap. Although there were several types of harps, each kind had a wooden frame with a sound box at the bottom, and strings made of animal gut. The lyre was an ancient kind of harp that was U-shaped and upright. Another kind was like our zither, which can rest flat on a person's lap. A third kind resembled a guitar.

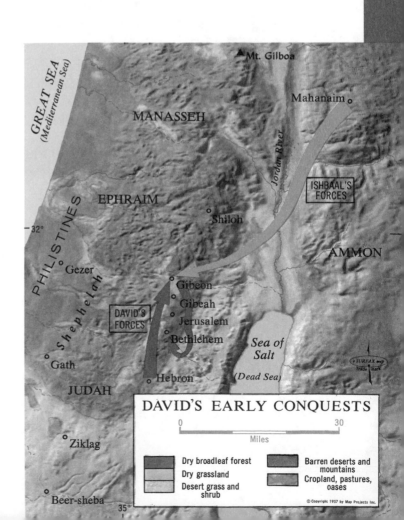

GREAT SEA (Mediterranean Sea)

Mt. Gilboa

MANASSEH

Mahanaim

ISHBAAL'S FORCES

EPHRAIM

Shiloh

Jordan River

PHILISTINES

—32°

Gezer

AMMON

Shephelah

Gibeon

Gibeah

DAVID'S FORCES

Jerusalem

Bethlehem

Sea of Salt

(Dead Sea)

Gath

Hebron

JUDAH

Ziklag

DAVID'S EARLY CONQUESTS

0 — 30

Miles

Dry broadleaf forest

Dry grassland

Desert grass and shrub

Barren deserts and mountains

Cropland, pastures, oases

Beer-sheba

35°

© Copyright 1957 by Map Projects Inc.

Heathen (p. 348)

A person who did not believe in the one God of the Israelites was called a heathen.

House of Judah (p. 367)

The House of Judah means the area in the southern part of the Holy Land that had been given as a dwelling place to the tribe of Judah. David was a member of the tribe of Judah, and was anointed king of the House of Judah before he became the king of other parts of the Holy Land.

Idolatry (p. 343)

Worshipping idols as gods is called idolatry. Many of the Israelites' neighbors in Canaan worshipped idols, so the Hebrews were surrounded by idolators and it was difficult to escape their influence. Some of the weaker souls among the Israelites turned to gods such as the Canaanites' Baal and the Philistines' Dagon. In doing so, they turned away from the God of Moses and the patriarchs.

Indicated by lot (p. 340)

The Israelites often chose lots to get an answer to a question. They used straws, pebbles, or sticks the way we flip a coin. The Israelites often used a pebble with a marking on one side. The pebble was thrown down and a yes or no answer determined by which side was up. The Israelites believed that God spoke to them and told them what to do when they chose lots.

Samuel chose lots to select Saul, the man God chose to be king. And later Saul chose lots to see who among his people had sinned. The lots said that the guilty one was either Saul or Jonathan, and that the other people were innocent. When Saul and Jonathan chose lots, Jonathan was indicated as the guilty one.

Javelin (p. 352)

A javelin was a spearlike weapon with a sharp metal point.

Judged Israel (p. 336)

When Samuel judged Israel, he decided which person was right in the disputes Israelites had with each other. Samuel was acting as judges do today, but instead of deciding according to city, state, and national laws, he decided according to the law of Moses. He traveled from place to place and held his court in various towns.

Samuel was different from the heroes and heroines of the Book of Judges, who were mainly fighters, and not judges in the same sense as Samuel.

"No razor shall touch his head" (p. 332)

Hannah was promising to God that her son's hair and beard would never be cut. This was called a "Nazirite vow" and meant that Samuel would always be set apart from other people. Wherever he went, people would know by his appearance that he had promised to be obedient to God.

Pillage (p. 350)

Pillage is robbery, usually committed by conquering soldiers in wartime.

Prophesied (p. 339)

Saul prophesied, or preached, warning the people to live as Moses had taught. When the prophets preached, the people believed their words were coming directly from God.

Prophets (p. 339)

Prophets were people who were called upon by God to strengthen the Israelites in the way of life taught by Moses. Today we think of a prophet as someone who can tell us what will happen in the future. This was not what the Hebrews meant by "prophet." The main task of the prophets was to point out wrongdoing and to call back to God those who had turned to idolatry. (See Idolatry.) The prophets often risked their lives by accusing powerful and important people of evil ways.

Sling (p. 349)

A sling was a long piece of braided woolen cord that was used for throwing stones. At the center of the sling's length there was a wide place where a stone was placed. The slinger, or person who used the sling, whirled it about above his head, cast the sling forward, and let the stone fly.

Shepherds used slings to protect their flocks and themselves against wild animals. Soldiers fought with slings made of leather, and slung balls made of flint.

Son of Belial (p. 361)

Calling someone a "son of Belial" was an insult. It meant "the son of nothingness" or "the son of things without value." By David's lifetime, the words had come to mean "the son of absolute evil."

Tabret (p. 352)

A tabret was a musical instrument that had to be struck to make a sound. It resembled a small drum or tambourine. "Tabret" was another name for the timbrel.

Tore his clothes (p. 367)

David tore his clothes to show his grief over the deaths of Saul and Jonathan. The Israelites had many ways of showing sorrow for their dead. In addition to tearing their clothing, they wore robes made of sackcloth, cut off their beards and hair, and put ashes on their heads and faces.

They also tore their clothing when they felt great anger or some other strong emotion.

Vow (p. 332)

A vow is a serious promise, made after considerable thought. The person who makes a vow is determined that it be kept at all costs.

"Your bone and your flesh" (p. 368)

This expression was used like our phrase, "your own flesh and blood." It means your own relatives.

Zion (p. 368)

Zion is a hill in Jerusalem. The Jebusites, whom David defeated, had a fort on Mount Zion. David made his home and began to build the city of Jerusalem around Mount Zion. The Hebrews thought of their city as "Zion," and had a deep affection for it. Later, when they were sent as prisoners of war to a strange country, they sang:

"By the waters of Babylon,
   there we sat down and wept
   when we remembered Zion."
                    (Psalm 137)